BG

AR PTS: 0.5

D1120220

MUSIC AND SOUND

Design	Cooper · West
Editor	Margaret Fagan
Researcher	Cecilia Weston-Baker
Illustrator	Louise Nevett
Consultant	J. W. Warren Ph.D. Formerly Reader in Physics Education, Department of Physics, Brunel University, London, U.K.

Designed and produced by
Aladdin Books Ltd
70 Old Compton Street
London W1

*First published in the
United States in 1987 by*
Gloucester Press
387 Park Avenue South
New York, NY 10016

ISBN 0-531-17034-9

Library of Congress Catalog
Card Number: 86-81373

Printed in Belgium

SCIENCE TODAY

MUSIC AND SOUND

Mark Pettigrew

GLOUCESTER PRESS
New York · Toronto · 1987

INTRODUCTION

Most of our lives are influenced by sound. Sound gives us information about the world around us. You can guess the weather from the sounds you hear: on a snowy day or when it is foggy, sounds are muffled. You can also guess where you are from the quality of the sounds you hear: for example, noises in a swimming pool produce an "echoing" sound. Many animals, including humans, make sounds deliberately to communicate, but even accidental sounds can give us useful information: the noise made by a falling tree warns us of danger nearby.

In this book you will find out how sounds are made, how you hear them and what makes each sound different.

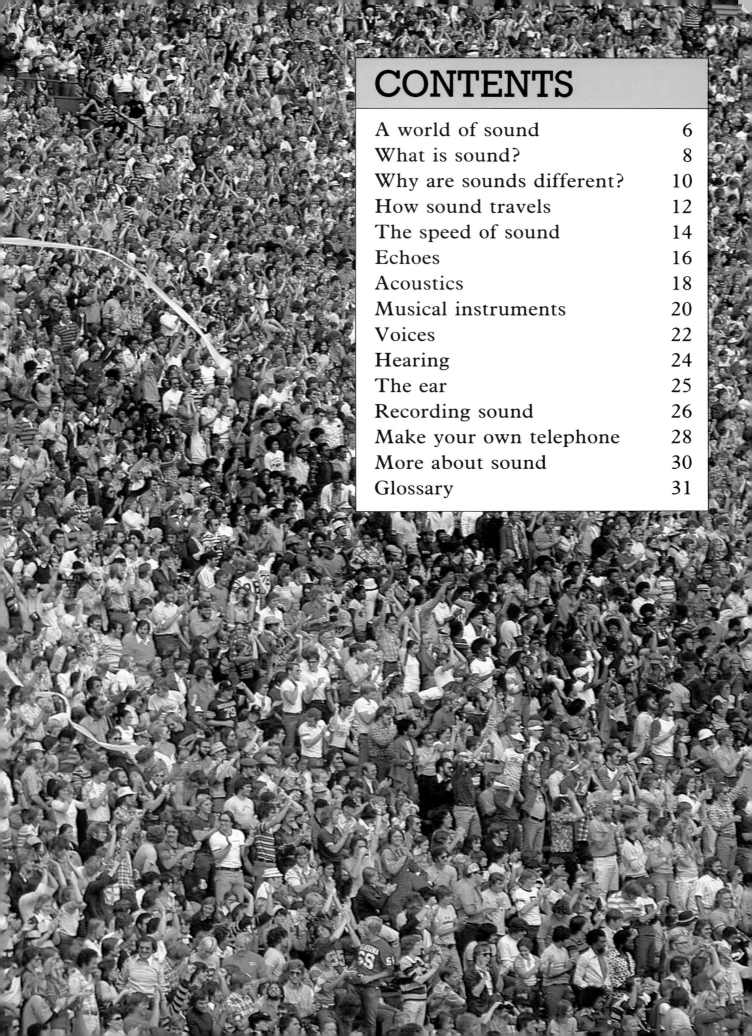

CONTENTS

A world of sound	6
What is sound?	8
Why are sounds different?	10
How sound travels	12
The speed of sound	14
Echoes	16
Acoustics	18
Musical instruments	20
Voices	22
Hearing	24
The ear	25
Recording sound	26
Make your own telephone	28
More about sound	30
Glossary	31

A WORLD OF SOUND

Sounds are all around us. Even at night when everything is still, we hear the sound of our own breathing or perhaps the noise of distant traffic. A lot of our information about the world comes from the quality of the sounds we hear. For example, some sounds are unpleasant because they carry an urgent message, like the cry of a hungry baby. Other sounds are more pleasant to our ears and help us to relax.

Sometimes we can even *feel* the effects of sound – we feel the effects of very loud music or an airplane taking off as vibrations in our bodies. In the case of an avalanche, we can *see* an effect of sound vibrations; a slight sound produces enough vibration to disturb a snow drift.

You can enjoy yourself listening to the music of groups like Duran Duran

A voice or a gunshot can produce enough vibrations to start an avalanche

WHAT IS SOUND?

Anything that vibrates – moves rapidly back and forth – produces a sound. For example, the buzzing of bees is caused by the movement of their wings vibrating the air about them hundreds of times a second. However, vibrations are usually much too fast to see, except as a blur. Things that make a very deep note, like the bottom notes on a piano, may only be vibrating about 30 times every second, but even this is too fast to see.

All sounds move energy from one place to another. When you beat a drum, the vibration of the drum makes the air near the drum vibrate. Vibrations spread quickly through the air and make parts of your ear vibrate. You hear the sound because energy has been transferred from the drum to your ear.

Sound vibrations
If you hold a ruler across the edge of a table and flick the end of it, the ruler vibrates and makes a sound. It is the vibration that produces the sound. When you move the ruler so that less of the ruler hangs over the table, the vibrations become faster and the sound changes.

The familiar sound of buzzing bees is produced by their wings beating

WHY ARE SOUNDS DIFFERENT?

We know that sounds are different from each other in many ways. For example, sounds can have a different "pitch," and the more rapid the vibrations, the higher the pitch. The number of vibrations produced every second is called the "frequency." As well as being rapid or slow, vibrations can be of different types. The "tone" of a sound is caused by the type of vibration making it. The smooth tone of a flute is due to very simple vibrations, whereas the tone of a buzzer is caused by complex, irregular vibrations.

Sounds can also start and finish in different ways. We say a sound like a drum beat, which starts quickly, has a very short "attack." A sound like a gong, which lingers before it disappears, has a long "decay."

Making musical notes

You can make a sound by blowing over the top of a milk bottle. This makes the air in the bottle vibrate. If you put different amounts of water in a series of milk bottles, you can make different musical notes. This is because smaller air spaces vibrate more rapidly.

Low notes

High notes

You can see the effects of a tuning fork's vibrations in water

HOW SOUND TRAVELS

Sound travels through the air by spreading out in a series of ripples, like ripples on a pond. These ripples are called "sound waves," and are caused by the air vibrating. In fact, sound can travel through any substance. This means that you can hear sounds underwater. You can even hear a sound traveling through wood if you put your ear to a tabletop and tap a spoon on the table.

On the Moon or in space, there is no air (or any other substance) to carry the vibrations. This means that the Moon is completely silent because sound cannot travel. Consequently, astronauts in space use radios to talk to each other. In an emergency, however, they could communicate by pressing their spacesuit helmets together. This would allow sound to travel as vibrations through their helmets and through the air inside.

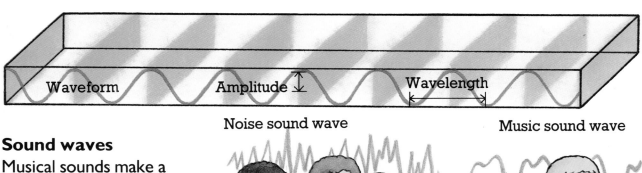

Waveform   Amplitude   Wavelength

Noise sound wave   Music sound wave

Sound waves
Musical sounds make a series of regular waves. The size of the vibration is called the "amplitude," and the distance between any two waves is called the "wavelength." Noise is like a mixture of lots of different sounds and it has no definite wavelength.

Astronauts communicate by radio while carrying out repairs

THE SPEED OF SOUND

When you see a starting pistol being fired some distance away, you hear the sound of the gun *after* you see the flash and the puff of smoke. This is because the speed of light (an astonishing 300 million meters, or 984 million feet, a second) is far faster than the speed of sound.

Sound travels through the air at a speed of about 330 meters (1,083 ft) per second. This means that it takes sound about three seconds to travel one kilometer (.6 miles) in air. However, sound travels faster in most other substances. Sound travels through steel, for example, at about six kilometers (3.7 miles) per second.

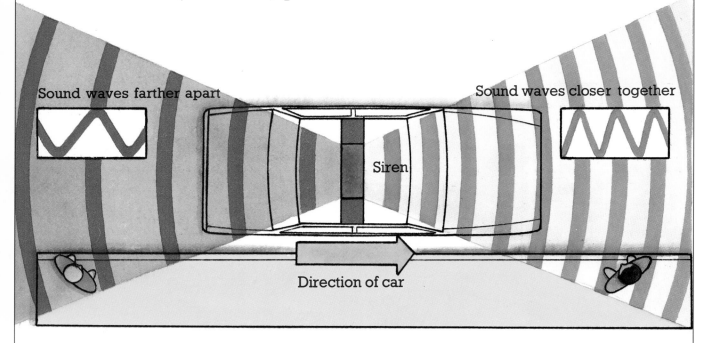

Sound waves farther apart   Sound waves closer together

Siren

Direction of car

The Doppler effect

As a police car passes with its siren sounding, you may have noticed that the sound you hear becomes lower in pitch. This is because sound waves in front of the car become "squashed" closer together. More vibrations reach your ear every second, and the note sounds higher. As the car drives away from you, fewer vibrations reach your ear, and the note sounds lower. This change in pitch is called the "Doppler effect."

THE SOUND BARRIER

When a plane approaches the speed of sound, it begins to "catch up" with the sound waves traveling away from it. As it passes the speed of sound, it breaks through the sound barrier and overtakes the sound it produces. As this happens, the sound spreads out as a "shock wave," which we hear as a sonic boom.

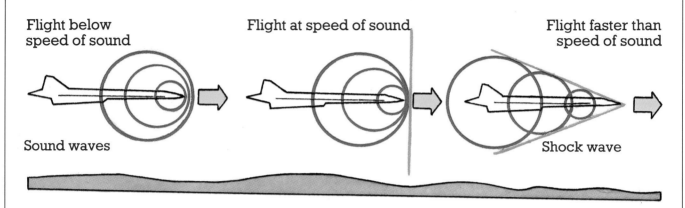

Flight below speed of sound

Flight at speed of sound

Flight faster than speed of sound

Sound waves

Shock wave

Concorde flies at speeds twice as fast as sound

ECHOES

We are used to the fact that sound usually travels in straight lines and spreads out in all directions. But if the sound hits a hard object, such as a cliff or a high wall, it can change direction. In fact, sound is "reflected" by a hard surface just as a beam of light is reflected by a mirror. If the surface is far away from the source of the sound, the sound is heard again a few seconds later as an echo.

Echoes can be used to examine the inside of someone's body without surgery. Very high frequency sound waves, called "ultrasound," are sent into the body. When these waves hit a surface inside the body, they are reflected and so produce an echo. The time it takes the echo to return builds up a picture of the inside of the body. Another device which uses echoes, called "sonar," measures the depth of the water by timing echoes from the sea bottom.

Sound waves sent out

Echo of sound waves

Sonar used by bats
Bats use a natural sort of sonar to detect their prey, usually insects. They send out a short, very high-pitched sound. This is reflected by the body of the prey. The bat's sensitive ears can hear the sonar echo and so tell what sort of animal is near, and where it is.

Ultrasound is used to produce an image of an unborn baby

ACOUSTICS

The harsh quality of sound you hear in empty rooms or swimming pools is caused by sound reflecting off bare walls and floors. The way music sounds when it is played in a church is due to the sound bouncing back and forth between opposite walls. By studying "acoustics" – how the quality of sound is affected by shape and materials – architects can design buildings that cut down the number of unwanted echoes. This is very important in the classroom, in a concert hall or in the theater, where every sound needs to be heard clearly.

Instead of being reflected by a surface, a sound may be "absorbed." The concert hall in the photograph has been designed using many materials that absorb sound, such as fabrics, carpets, plastic and wood.

Absorbing sound
The sound of an alarm clock ringing travels through the air and reaches your ear easily. However, if you put the clock under your pillow much of the sound will be *absorbed* and very little sound travels to your ear. This makes the alarm sound muffled.

Sydney Opera House, Australia, is designed to absorb unwanted sound

MUSICAL INSTRUMENTS

Anything you play to produce a musical sound – a series of notes – is a musical instrument. You can produce musical sounds using very simple instruments. For example, if you stretch a piece of wire between two nails on a wooden board and "pluck" the wire, you hear a sound. You can change the pitch of the sound by pulling the wire tighter. This is the way that string instruments work. Wind instruments work by making a tube full of air vibrate, like blowing across a milk bottle.

As well as containing something which vibrates, nearly all musical instruments have something to "amplify" the sound, or make it louder. The amplification may be achieved by the shape of the instrument, or there may be a "sound box" to amplify the sound, as in a guitar.

String
String instruments have wires stretched across them. The pitch is changed by pulling the wires tighter.

Wind
Wind instruments are played by vibrating your lips at one end of a tube. To change the pitch, you change the length of tube.

Percussion
Most percussion instruments are played by hitting them. Most can produce notes of only one pitch.

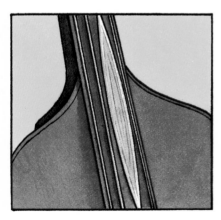

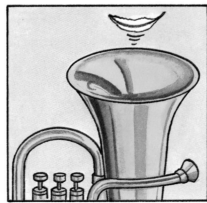

The orchestra is divided into string, wind and percussion sections

VOICES

People use their voices from a very early age. However, it takes many years to learn to speak properly. Speaking and singing are done by blowing air from the lungs past two ligaments, called the "vocal cords," in the voicebox, or "Adam's apple." By moving your mouth and tongue you can make different sounds. The pitch of the sound is controlled by the vocal cords.

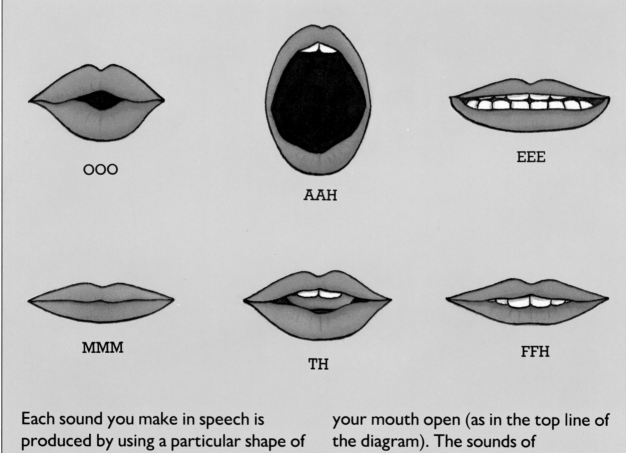

OOO

AAH

EEE

MMM

TH

FFH

Each sound you make in speech is produced by using a particular shape of your mouth and lips. In fact, these shapes are so precise that deaf people can learn to lip-read. The sounds of vowels are made with your mouth open (as in the top line of the diagram). The sounds of consonants are made by using your lips, tongue, or teeth to close your mouth slightly (bottom line of diagram).

Some animals, like dogs and monkeys, make sounds in the same way as humans, although they cannot learn to make such a variety of sounds. Many animals make sounds to communicate in other ways. For example, grasshoppers make a noise by rubbing their legs on their wings. Rabbits thump a hind leg on the ground to make a sound warning of danger. Most sounds made by animals carry a message, like "keep away" or "here I am."

Hungry birds call for food

HEARING

Most people can hear sounds from about 20 to about 18,000 vibrations per second. The exact range varies from person to person, and as we get older our ability to hear high notes decreases.

Many animals have ears that can hear sounds outside the range of human hearing. For example, rabbits have a larger outer ear to help them hear quieter sounds and so alert them to danger.

Animals use their ears to tell them the direction of sound. They do this by "comparing" the amounts of sound reaching each ear. Knowing the direction of sound is important for their survival and for hunting. Some animals, for example, foxes and rabbits, move their ears to pinpoint the exact direction of sound.

Many animals use their sense of hearing to hunt

THE EAR

The part of your ear that you can see is called the outer ear. It collects sound waves over a large area and channels them down the ear canal. This amplifies the sound. Sound waves reach the ear drum and make it vibrate. The vibrations then travel to the inner ear after moving three small bones in the middle ear. In the inner ear, an organ called the "cochlea" sends nerve messages to the brain for every sound the ear receives.

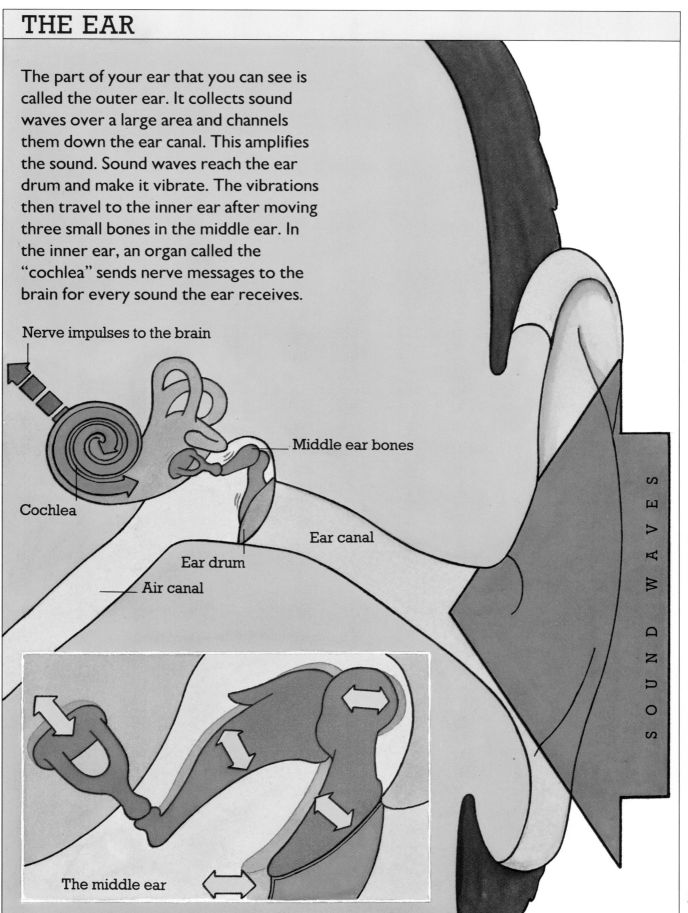

Nerve impulses to the brain

Cochlea

Middle ear bones

Ear canal

Ear drum

Air canal

SOUND WAVES

The middle ear

RECORDING SOUND

For a long time people have been recording sounds either by writing them down as words, or by writing down musical notes. However, by using records and tape recorders we can also record the *actual* sounds we hear.

Until recently, records all used an irregular groove formed in a flat piece of plastic. A narrow stylus follows the groove as the record turns and remakes the original pattern of vibrations. Today's compact disks use patterns of microdots instead of a groove.

Tape recorders use the pattern of sound vibrations to make changes in a magnetic coating on a plastic tape. A microphone converts sound vibrations to electric signals which can then be stored electronically in a record or tape.

A microphone

A microphone uses the energy in sound waves to produce electric signals. The sound waves hit a thin piece of plastic, called a diaphragm, and make it vibrate. This makes a small magnet vibrate inside a coil of fine wire, which produces a series of electric signals.

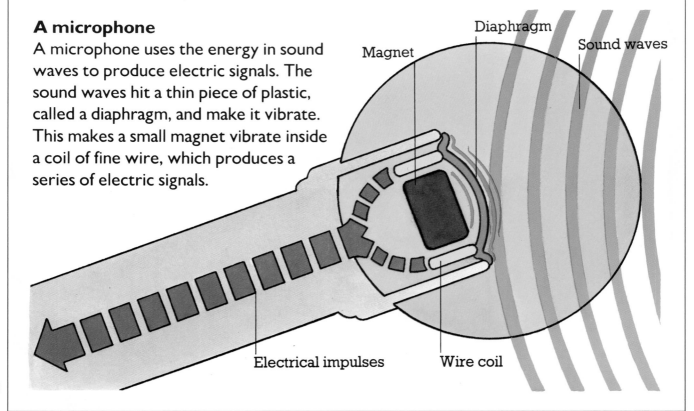

Diaphragm

Magnet

Sound waves

Electrical impulses

Wire coil

Sounds picked up by a microphone are recorded electronically in a studio

MAKE YOUR OWN TELEPHONE

Telephones are a vital communication link. By
making this simple telephone, you can discover
that a telephone works by transmitting vibrations.
In this model the tracing paper acts as a
diaphragm which vibrates to the sound of your
voice.

What you need
A cardboard tube, two elastic bands,
tape, string, tracing paper, two
matchsticks.

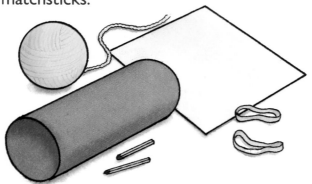

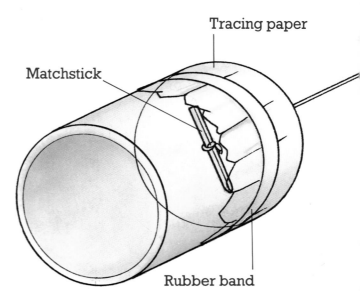

Tracing paper

Matchstick

Rubber band

1. Cut the cardboard tube in half.

3. Cut off a long length of string. Fasten it to each tube by pricking a hole in the tracing paper and threading it through. Then, tie each end of the string to a matchstick to hold it in place.

2. Cut out a square of tracing paper and wrap it around the top of each tube, as shown. Attach the tracing paper to the tube with a rubber band and hold it in position with tape.

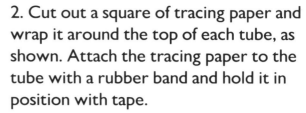

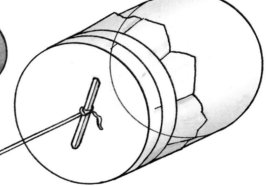

String

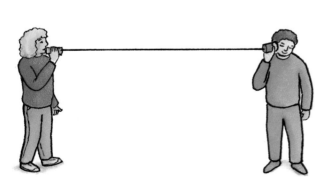

How the telephone works

Sound vibrations produced by your voice travel down the length of string, as long as the string is held taut. This enables you to use your telephone to talk to a friend some distance away. As you speak into one end of the telephone, the diaphragm vibrates. These vibrations travel along the string and make the tracing paper at the other end vibrate in the same way. If your friend holds the other cardboard tube to his ear, he will be able to hear your message clearly.

MORE ABOUT SOUND

How we measure sound

The pitch, or frequency, of a sound can be measured by counting the number of vibrations happening every second. It is measured in "hertz." The note called middle "C" has a frequency of 261 hertz. The tone of a note cannot be measured, but it can be studied using a device called an "oscilloscope" which lets us look at the pattern of vibration of a sound.

Decibel levels

The loudness of a sound is measured in "decibels." The louder the sound is, the higher the decibel level. Louder sounds transfer more energy, but surprisingly an increase of only three decibels means that a sound carries twice as much energy. Sound above 130 decibels is produced by vibrations that are strong enough to produce permanent damage to your hearing.

Pain threshold

200

150

100

50

0

Decibels

Rustling leaves · Normal conversation · Vacuum cleaner · Heavy traffic · Pneumatic drill · Military jet · Space rocket

GLOSSARY

Acoustics
The science dealing with the nature of sound.

Amplify
To make a sound louder.

Amplitude
The size of a vibration, which is related to the loudness of a sound.

Doppler effect
The way the pitch of a sound is changed if the thing making the sound is moving fast. The Doppler effect can be used to measure how fast something is moving.

Frequency
The number of vibrations every second in a sound. Frequency is measured in hertz.

Noise
A sound made up of many different frequencies, and which contains no main frequency.

Pitch
The quality of a note that makes it sound deep or high. It depends on the frequency of the vibration causing the sound.

Sonar
A method of measuring distance, which measures the time for an echo to return from an object and uses that to work out how far away the object is.

Sound box
A hollow box with an opening, placed behind something making a sound in order to amplify the sound.

Speed of sound
The speed of sound is about 330 meters (1,083 ft) per second in air. In other substances, the speed of sound is often higher.

Tone
The quality of a sound which, for example, tells you the difference between a whistle and a buzzer.

Ultrasound
Very high frequency sound waves, too high for humans to hear.

Vibration
A rapid, repeated movement back and forth, causing a sound.

Vocal cords
The flaps of ligaments in your voicebox. They produce sounds as air from the lungs is blown over them.

Waveform
A way to draw the pattern of vibrations causing a sound. Vibrations are shown as up and down movements of a line.

Wavelength
The distance between the same point on any two waves of a sound traveling through a substance.

INDEX

A
acoustics 18, 19, 31
air 8, 10, 12, 14
amplification 20, 25, 31
amplitude 12, 31
animals 16, 23, 24

C
communication 12, 13, 23, 28, 29

D
decibel level 30
Doppler effect 14, 31

E
ear, the 8, 12, 14, 18, 25
echoes 16, 18
energy 8, 26, 30

F
frequency 10, 30, 31

H
hearing 6, 12, 14, 15, 24, 30
hertz 30, 31

M
musical instruments 8, 10, 12, 20, 21
musical notes 8, 10, 20, 24, 26, 30, 31

N
noise 6, 12, 31

O
orchestra 21
oscilloscope 30

P
pitch 10, 14, 20, 22, 30, 31

R
radios 12, 13
recordings 26, 27

S
shock waves 15
silence 12
sonar 16, 31
sonic boom 15
sound barrier 15
sound box 20, 31

sound waves 12, 14, 15, 16, 25, 26
speech 22, 30
speed of sound 14, 15, 31

T
telephones 28, 29
tone 10, 30, 31

U
ultrasound 16, 17, 31

V
vibration 6, 12, 14, 20, 24, 25, 26, 28, 30, 31
vocal cords 22, 31
voices 22, 28, 29

W
waveform 12, 31
wavelength 12, 31

Acknowledgments
Cover, contents page and pages 6, 7, 15, 19 and 25: Tony Stone Associates; title page and page 21: Zefa; pages 9 and 23: Art Directors; page 11: Robert Harding; page 13: Science Photo Library; pages 17 and 22: Colorific; page 28: Cooper·West